BODY LANGUAGE
MASTERY

Become A Master Of Reading People With Body Language.
Find Out All The Essentials To Improve Your Life With
Nonverbal Communication

BENEDICT GOLEMAN

and brands within this book are for clarifying purposes only and are the property of the owners themselves, not affiliated with this document.

Table of Contents

Introduction

To 'read' people is to quickly look at their different features, expressions, adorations, and anything else that is connected to them, to determine accurately what kind of a person they are. People are only a representation of the environment they exist in, and everything that can be physically seen and judged is likely to be an explanation for someone's inner character. In a lot of ways, the focal point of 'reading' people is not to determine who they are entirely and write a thesis on it, but rather just at that moment to determine the signaling that person is doing. By signaling what we mean is that in different kinds of clothing, makeup, or expressions, we can determine what people are trying to communicate with other people around them subtly.

Of course, nobody would wear an expensive ring unless they wanted to virtue signal everyone about their beauty, riches, taste, and whatnot, so by reading these things, you can at least determine how people want to be perceived in different situations and settings. It might not tell you who they are entire as a person of course, but you will be able to see people for what they want to be seen as, and that reveals a lot of information about people; you can see all the needs people are trying to fulfill, all the insecurities they are trying to cover up, and all their desires and motivations.

Now, the most important aspect of understanding how to read people is to learn to read yourself. All knowledge and understanding that we have come from experience, so if you haven't experienced something, you might get it, but it will be hard for you to understand it. It's only when you can study yourself and how you function that you will be able to understand similar things in other people. So, the first step in trying to understand others and analyze them is to analyze yourself.

Knowledge of the self can never be complete; the whole purpose of the brain is to hide from you so that you can function without getting crippled by self-doubt, past trauma, or things about yourself you may not particularly like. This journey towards self-awareness is not simple, it will take ages, you might never even reach the end, and eventually, it's just going to make things more complicated rather than simplifying them. So, be careful about what you're getting into and prepare yourself mentally.

Learning to cultivate self-awareness is pretty simple, and doesn't require much effort since the only thing it involves is reflecting on your past, different events and stimuli you had to go through, and how those things affected the formation of your 'self.' If you want to know about yourself, first, you must let go of the lie that you do know yourself because, as humans, all of us function under different forms of consciousness that alienate us from who we are.

A deeper analysis requires you to look at how you would describe yourself, and you will realize that people tend to look at themselves as only objects that have certain features embedded into them, that are as solid as a rock, and do not change, which of course, is a lie. Most people describe themselves using generic features that do not explain anything about them; they say they are friendly, emotional, extroverted, cynical, etc.—these words can be used to describe anybody on earth, and they are words people use to deflect from telling people who they are. If a random stranger asked you who you are, these are probably the words you will use because you do not want them to know information about you that might give them a deeper insight into your behavior.

These unchanging features are reductive; they are unchanging, rigid, and common across the whole human population. If you would use these words to describe yourself too, then you might have to rethink how much you know about yourself and if like everyone else, you've been avoiding describing who you are by hiding behind these generic words. Human beings are dynamic, they change every day, and their qualities develop depending on the environment they are a part of. There isn't a single set of explanatory words with no real meaning that can describe them.

Imagine your life is just like a car. Every car model comes with a particular specification that makes it different from other models. Once you understand the specifications of your car model, the next step is for you to know how your car can get along with other cars on the highway. This knowledge will enable you to get maximum performance from your car since you know its strengths and weaknesses when compared to other models. Studies show that people who learned how to properly analyze others have become a better spouse, manager, worker and even better parents.

Over the centuries, we have learned how to utilize this knowledge to help shape our decisions. We have made it second nature to always try to delve beneath the surface—beneath the smile or anger. Analyzing people is an indispensable skill you need to acquire.

It is the determining factor in so many aspects of our daily activities. Have you ever marveled at how some people are so good at negotiations while others are not? Perhaps you wonder why some are so great at building rapport with their colleagues in the office while others can't seem to connect. You might think this is because of their smooth way of talking. Perhaps you will have a change of mind if you realize that verbal communication makes up only 7 percent of effective communication while body language communication takes up a whopping 50 percent. These "successful" people have discovered how to interpret others' body language and how to project the right body language to others. It is called decoding when you can "properly" analyze people's body language, and it is encoding when you have learned how to send the right body language cues. But don't worry, as we will go in-depth into the two definitions within this book. If you paid close attention, you would notice the word properly is in quotes. It is a well-known fact that some people are good at picking nonverbal cues from the body language of the other party. This set of individuals, in psychology, are termed as having a high "mind-reading motivation" (MRM). Despite having a high MRM, this set of individuals are prone to make wrong assertions or guesses from the nonverbal cues.

On the other hand, those with low "mind-reading motivation" often blunder through their world without a clue on how to harness the nonverbal cues of those around them. Therefore, it is necessary to know how to properly read and analyze people since this can make a lot of difference to the actualization and success of your life goals. It is the difference between those who excel in their daily activities and those who don't.

Understanding Body Language

First off, I want to ask you a question, is body language we are born with or something we learn?

I don't expect you to have an answer because this question is pretty hard to answer because of two things.

First, body language is something that is evolved with time to match the social needs of humans. Some scientists and anthropologists study which gestures have developed and why we need them.

Secondly, within communication, body language can be divided into several different groups. There are some reactions and gestures that we are born with, and they are universal signals around the world. Others we learn through observation and become refined with use and age.

So, really, the answer to the question is, it depends. For example, you weren't taught to scowl when you are angry. This was a programmed response in your brain of how to act when you feel angry. On the other hand, you have learned with time that standing up straight and smiling will project a positive image.

There is another question that some people like to ask, and that is, "Since we have words, do we really need body language? Aren't we able to communicate without it?" The truth is that the use of speech is still a fairly new thing to human communication. Before we learned verbal communication, our communication skills were a lot like that of other animals, which was made up of non-verbal cues.

As you have probably heard, "old habits die hard," so that means body language still plays a very big part in our communication process, whether you want it to or not.

This can easily be seen when a person is speaking on the phone. While the person on the other end of the line can't see you, you probably still move around, wave your hands, and make facial expressions to stress your point. While it could seem primitive, during the time before we understood language, waving and grunting was enough to help us drive home a point.

You can't have true communication face to face without some type of body language. Verbal and nonverbal communications are two sides of the same coin. View body language as the "spice" that comes along with the main dish. You can say "I'm fine" in several ways with different facial expressions and tones, and every time it is going to affect the message.

Body language is non-verbal communication where physical actions are used to express a person's feelings. These actions include eye movement, touch, and use of space, gestures, posture, and facial expressions. Body language is present in humans as well as animals.

The Importance of Body Language

Body language is an extremely important part of the communication process that few have studied. It makes up most of our communication and tends to be more accurate than the things we say.

Everybody has heard that actions speak louder than words, and this is so true because there are a lot of things that we communicate without ever saying a word. A simple shrug can tell a person, "I'm not sure." Raising your eyebrows can mean, "Did I hear that right?" Turning your palms face up and shrugging your shoulders could mean, "I'm not sure what I should do." A simple point to the nose means, "That's right."

The body reinforces the things that we say. A person could say, "I'm not sure," or they could also turn the hands up, raise their eyebrows, frown a bit, and poke out their bottom lip. This will make a person laugh and help to relieve a bit of pressure if the situation is tense.

Why should a person take the time to learn the imprecise meanings of body language? Technically, the unconscious mind is already an expert at it, and the unconscious mind is more powerful than that of the conscious mind. Why should we use our time and hard work to take this from our unconscious mind and move into the conscious mind, make this confusing, struggling with understanding it, before simply pushing it back into the unconscious mind after we stop focusing on it with the conscious mind?

I'm glad you asked.

This needs to be done because it gives us the chance to develop the skill of reading another person and control our own body language. This means that you can communicate with intent instead of leaving things to chance.

For example, when we first meet a person, the unconscious mind begins to develop answers to questions that we have learned are important. Are they going to hurt me? Are they bigger than me? Could they be a potential mate? Do they understand what they are saying? As the relationship begins to grow, the big question of trust comes up.

When you communicate with intent, you can use your body language to create some type of trust with other people more quickly and in a reliable way instead of leaving it up to the unconscious mind. This is a great skill for a salesperson, but professional speakers can use it as well. The audience wants to trust the person they see on stage, and being able to do this will help that audience buy into what the speaker is trying to say.

The best way to improve the odds and speed of trust building is to start mirroring what the other person is doing. This is something that has been studied a lot and is an odd phenomenon. You can look around you and see people unconsciously mirroring other people, and then they easily agree on things. This is how the body tells one another, "Hey, we act the same way; we agree on things, we are both on the same page."

This doesn't have to be unconscious, though. You can consciously mirror a stranger, which will help to improve their depth and rate of trust-building. This should carefully be done, but it is rare for a person to call you out on it unless you start to become hyperactive in your movements and try to mirror every single twitch.

How can speakers use this? How can a speaker mirror an audience? There are a couple of ways that they could do this. First off, they can align themselves by walking into the crowd and facing the stage as if they were an audience member. Second, if they are given a chance to interact with them, like a Q & A, they can mirror the person who is asking the question. Thirdly, they can act something out and ask the audience to participate. It should be something that is relevant, though. The speaker will only create more questions if they make their audience do jumping jacks for no reason.

It's hard work to use body language consciously for psychological purposes, but the things you get in return by making stronger connections are worth it; furthermore, through the act of reading body language. However, it is interesting to note that there are uncommon signs of lying.

There are some people who will clear their throats a lot, some change the pitch of their voice, or they stutter. Some may even try to take your attention to something else or they try to stall the conversation. Foot tapping, face rubbing, looking away, blushing, or raising their shoulders can indicate that they aren't comfortable within the conversation. But these are only a few things that we will look at later on.

Body language also helps us to express our feelings clearly. When you start looking at nonverbal signals, it will help you figure out how the other person actually feels about their words. For example, somebody could say 'yes' to something, but their body language says that they aren't really interested. This is great for a person in a leadership or managerial position so that they know who would be best for certain job assignments. If their heart isn't into it, they will likely not do their best.

With job interviews, body language is something of the main factor. If the person shows ease and confidence in their body language, they have a great chance of getting the job. Like we have said, body language can make a person seem uncomfortable or out of control. This will make an applicant appear less confident and comfortable.

When you talk to a person, their body language can tell you if they are actually listening or careless. Leaning forward shows interest. Leaning back might mean that they aren't interested or feel as if they are superior to you. If a person is positioned close to you and leaning forward as they are talking, it could mean that they are trying to talk you into something or dominate the conversation. If a person is talking to you and won't make eye contact, you will come off as uninterested and just wait for your turn to speak. This will make you appear as if you don't care and they probably won't want to listen to you speak.

Some body languages are easier to interpret than others, and this is simply a fact that you will figure out throughout the remainder of this book.

Body Language in History

There are gestures, like the "manual rhetoric" of the Roman orators and the general mannerism of the entire body, that have been studied since Classical times. During the fourth century BCE in Greece, the upperclassmen kept what was considered a "firm" stance and an unhurried walk where they took long strides. This made them appear as people of leisure, which set them apart from slaves and artisans who always had to hurry to get things done. It also worked to separate them from women as well who walked in a mincing manner and took small steps. The courtesans of the time would sway their hips as they walked. In Ancient Rome, strictly controlled and limited gestures made a person look in control, which was required for orators and aristocrats.

Writings about body language were prevalent during the Renaissance. The physiognomists of the 17th century, such as Charles Lebrun and Giovanni Della Porta organized the facial expressions of different emotions and characters. There investigations on gestures, and the investigations of their contemporaries John Bulwer and Giovanni Bonifacio, were conducted by assuming there was a universal language of gesture and expression, which people could assume and understand all around the world.

The chances are that the practical study of nonverbal communication started with actors. This is especially true during the 19th century when silent movies were first shown. Actors learned how to properly display feelings, status, and attitude by mimicking their characters' body language, which is no small feat.

The amazing things are that it is easy to understand and connect with the character even though there are no words or voices. This goes to show how powerful and relevant body language actually is.

Who was the first person to really study body language and its origins?

Charles Darwin, the father of evolution, was the first person to start studying animals and humans' body language in the book The Expression of the Emotions of Man and Animals in 1872. Through careful observation, he found that humans, much like animals, shared inborn behaviors that everybody used. These cues were able to reveal internal emotions or were able to help communicate with people.

The physical conditions that people had to live in, their bodily movements, and their habitual actions all had some sort of consequence on the structure of their body. This was discovered by paleo-archaeologists who used excavated skeletons to offer some thoughts about past body habits. There are some modern zoologists and ethnologists like Desmond Morris, who stress the similarities of body movements between animals and humans when expressing dominance, fear, and hostility.

Through his book, he pretty much established the science of body language. The majority of observations and studies made today started with his studies.

The biggest parts of the study of non-verbal communication began, oddly enough, during the 1960s. Since that time, it has become a significant part of different sciences like psychiatry, social science, anthropology, and business.

Albert Mehrabian

In the late '60s, Albert Mehrabian performed many experiments to figure out how important gestures and intonation were when sharing messages. He found that about seven percent of our communication took place verbally. 39% of it he called paraverbal, which means tone and intonation, and the remaining 55% was nonverbal. This means that the movement of our body, hands, and other simple gestures are very important in the way that we communicate.

People do sometimes debate these results because they came from a controlled experiment and didn't reflect what would be considered a realistic setting. But it was able to give Mehrabian a chance to show the words alone will not provide us with enough information to understand a message.

Intonation

Intonation refers to the varying pitch of a person's voice when they speak. Let's think about the word 'thanks.' This is typically seen as a positive word, right? However, if somebody were to say 'thanks' in a firm or curt tone, how are you going to feel? You probably aren't going to interpret it in a positive way, and you probably won't believe that they are thankful at all. Intonation is a big part of how we convey emotions.

Facial expressions and intonation tend to be very similar across cultures. You can pretty much figure out when a person is disgusted no matter where you are in the world. In a similar manner, happiness and sadness are typically the same the world over.

Gestures and Movements

Gestures are a person's way of conveying the subtle parts of a message. Gestures can even take the place of entire words. For example, if you want a person to continue talking because what they are saying is interested, you won't cut them off and say, "That's cool! Keep talking." You will likely lean forward to let them know you are interested in the things they are saying or nod your head. Most of our gestures involve our hands. In the US, hello tends to be said with a wave. A thumb up is used to say everything is good, or, if a person were to become extremely upset, we can use our middle finger. We can even display impatience with our hands.

Differences in Cultures

The modern study of body language is based on assuming that gestures aren't universal or natural. Instead, they are the products of culture and social influence. The likeness between facial expressions of chimps to show fear and subordination, and the smile of a human, can help to show the difference and the similarities between two primate species.

Anthropologists, like Marcel Mauss, have shown that even the smallest parts of physical activity, like how a person sits, walks, sleeps, or eats, seem to be affected by their culture and vary between societies. This not only includes deliberate signals people use for communication but also involuntary reactions, such as weeping or blushing.

Actions that may seem instinctive or spontaneous, when looked at closely are neither transparent nor spontaneous. To some degree, they are ordered, formalized and stylized to a certain code, which could mean nothing in different cultures, places or contexts. The person who jumps to their feet, smiles and hugs another person may create some kind of discomfort or offense to a person who is not familiar with this type of greeting. The action of simply nodding the head as you walk past may not have the same effect on a person who isn't used to displaying public acknowledgments.

Modern Studies

The majority of people who study body language are social psychologists, linguists, and anthropologists. The science of body language is kinesics. Their studies include the ways and frequency with which others touch people when they talk and the distance they have during their interactions. Linguists have called gestures another form of language, possibly even the predecessor of language. They have studied several forms of kinesics communication used by different groups and cultures, like clergy, stockbrokers, and beggars.

Surveys across cultures show the variability of gestures and expressions are supplemented by what travelers experience when they go to different countries, or even things seen in movies and heard in music from different areas of the world. There is a chance that with long-distance travel in the late 20th century and the globalization of culture, some differences have started to diminish. The homogenization of cultures can happen quickly in different aspects, like fashion, foods, or using foreign words or decorations. But it takes more time when it comes to gestures and expressions, which people take longer to absorb and change.

Body language is not only the most fundamental and basic form of expression used by humans, but it is also a very sophisticated and culturally specific form of signals where movements and expressions play as much a part as speech, for example, the group of grimaces of displeasure at an unpleasant sensation, the timing of bows between Japanese of equal rank, and the series of insulting hand gestures shared by angry drivers in Brazil.

Chapter 1: Extravert or Introvert?

Let us look at some of the clues that will help you differentiate whether you are dealing with an introvert or an extravert.

Body Language

This is the first thing that you will notice about someone when you need them.

Extraverted people have a high level of energy, something that is easily seen in conversations. When extroverts talk, they are usually more energetic compared to introverts. They will use a lot of body language just to express a few thoughts and emphasize them. You will notice they use a lot of body movements, mostly hand movements and facial expressions.

On the other hand, introverts are more reserved when it comes to energy. Instead of expending a lot of energy, they will seek to conserve the energy. They are usually not in a hurry, and they opt for a quiet disposition.

You will notice these changes better when they are in groups. Extraverts will become noisier as time goes by, while introverts will tend to be quiet and retreat to a corner and watch the proceedings.

Style of Communication

You will notice a lot of differences in communication between the two personality types.

The extrovert usually makes most of the talking, and they are loud as well. When a topic comes up, the extravert starts talking before understanding whether the question is directed.

On the other hand, you will notice that introverts don't engage in a lot of talks, and when asked a question, they take some time to think about it first before they respond. If you interact with an introvert, you will notice a lot of awkward silences between conversations.

When it comes to volume, extroverts are usually noisier compared to introverts. They are more vocal and tend to escalate their volume, especially when they are more than one in a group. Woe unto you if you find yourself in the company of more than two extraverts because each one will be trying to sound louder than the other.

Conversely, you will find introverts keen to listen to the conversations and contribute only when asked to. But such chances are rare because extroverts rarely give someone else time to talk.

Appearance

This might not be the strongest clue yet, but it can help you to emphasize some of the clues that you already have. Usually, extroverts tend to try and call more attention to themselves than they deserve. They might wear clothes that are brighter, drive fashionable cars while on the other hand introverts are usually seen in more subtle colors and don't go for the spotlight.

The Level of Interaction Sought

Usually, extroverts will seek and tend to enjoy a higher level of social interaction as compared to introverts.

For extraverts, you will find them tagging along with friends to date with their spouse or a worker that will always wait for the whole group to finish work so that they eat together.

On the other hand, you will notice that introverts don't wish to identify with other people. They tend to sit alone all the time and never show up for functions and parties unless it is necessary to do so.

Extroverts are more likely to approach and engage strangers as compared to their introverted colleagues.

The Occupation

On many occasions, you will find that the occupation will give you a very useful clue.

But keep in mind that making assumptions based only on someone's occupation can mislead you because some people have jobs that don't take their talents into focus.

So, if you decide to perform speed-reading on a person based on the occupation, you need to take into account the various stereotypes that you have observed over the years.

The good thing is that before you put the system in place, you get to talk for some time with the person you are putting under scrutiny.

When you decide to look at occupation, you need to ask some questions such as how the person decided to get into the line of work, whether they love their job, and if there are a few aspects they don't like about the job.

They also need to tell you what they would have preferred to do instead of the job.

These questions will make you know if the person is satisfied with the job they are doing, or they are just trying to survive.

At the time, most people get into an occupation just to make some money. When you go out to judge someone depending on their occupation, you need to put in mind that most of the workers aren't suited to their jobs.

Ask if this is the case before you go ahead to judge them.

You also need to understand what constitutes job satisfaction for both extraverts and introverts

In general, extroverts are comfortable in a job that allows them to interact with many people, handle many projects, and be free with their ideas.

On the other hand, introverts desire to work in a job where they focus on a project. They also flourish in jobs whereby they think things through and work steadily.

Some jobs and careers are known to attract extroverts, while others are known to attract introverts.

Introverts opt for computer programming, artists, libraries, bookkeeping, and accounting.

Jobs that attract extraverts include marketing, managerial, acting, PR, social work, and public speaking.

Interests and Hobbies

When it comes to extracurricular activities, there are sports that attract extroverts and those that attract introverts.

Introverts love games that are more individualistic in nature, such as running, swimming, golf, and tennis. Extraverts opt for games that gravitate towards teams such as football and the like.

If you decide to consider sports, you need to consider how they do sports and not what they do. While both types of personalities enjoy playing sports, they usually do it in different ways.

Sensor vs. Intuitive

The Percentage of the Population
Studies show that nearly 65% of the population in America is made of sensors, while the remainder is intuitive.

So, when you are interacting with someone, you will most likely be talking to a Sensor.

Chapter 2: The Communication Style

One of the best parts of reading someone is the way of communicating.

Sensors communicate in a straightforward manner, while intuitive ones tend to complicate their communication most of the time.

Intuitive will tend to take a lot of time to say something simple.

Sensing

Just like the name suggests, Sensors live their lives in a real way.

Before they take a step, they usually absorb anything around them to take the next step based on facts. They put a lot of emphasis on getting the right information before they can make a choice. Using these facts, they usually calculate the best practical course of action to take.

Sensors also take advantage of knowledge and experience. For them, the past is a wealth of wisdom and lessons that they can draw inspiration from. They take all the information and then factor it into their decision-making process. They also do things in a step-by-step manner.

Sensors are good at learning and remembering a large number of facts and figures that they use in school. They are organized, and this makes them a valuable addition to any team. Due to the use of facts, employers appreciate their ability to take fast actions and be decisive in all they do.

Intuitive, on the other hand, don't have the time to look at facts; instead, they work with a lot of uncertainty. They also have the capacity to take information and data, but they don't use them to make decisions at all.

What matters most to intuitives is the bigger picture, and they don't let some tiny details determine the decision they make in the future. They don't look so much to the present, but they try to dream and create many possibilities for the future.

They have the ability to spot decisions and opportunities early, making them very valuable to some industries.

These are a few examples of how you can speed-read someone depending on their profiles. You need to understand how to differentiate the various personalities so that you can read someone's mind very fast.

Temperament

We have looked at the different clues that you can use to identify the different types, but you need more than this to speed-read someone—you need to check out the temperament.

You need to understand the different types of temperaments to be able to speed read someone.

Traditionalists

These embrace the different rules and responsibilities that have been put down, and they do this so that they can do the right thing regardless of the situation.

They value orderliness, stability, reliability, and consistency. They are always hardworking and serious. When they promise something, count on them that they will do as they promised.

So, how can you speed-read traditionalists? You will realize that they respect the time set and stick to a schedule like clockwork. They are always prepared and will stay on the task, however long it takes.

That is always present when you need them, and if they aren't present, they always try to make it to the place of work within the shortest time possible.

They always try to respond to any question that you give them, and they will listen keenly then respond in the right way. When you assign them a task, you will be amazed because they do what you ask them to do always.

Experiencers

This desire to be active and enjoy all the freedom that they want.

When they work, they usually put all their effort into the ability to accomplish what can be done within a certain time limit. They like challenges and will move from one to the other.

So, how do you speed-read experiencers? First, you will realize that the person is easygoing and casual, which makes the experience of working with them very enjoyable. They usually expect you to ask them questions which they will answer diligently. Additionally, they give practical tips so that you don't have to wonder so much what they are saying.

When faced with a situation, they try to make the explanation as easy as possible so that you don't have to query. They even take time to clarify the next action steps without being too formal or too pushy.

Conceptualizers

Just like the name suggests, this kind of person uses concepts to make decisions.

They are all about being excellent in all they do, and they are usually pushed to get knowledge then set high standards both for themselves and the people they work with. They think strategically, and they are very good problem solvers.

How to speed-read conceptualizers is easy? First, you will notice that they usually look at the bigger picture and not just what will happen in a few hours. They also expect you to support any decision you make with logic. They also have very good problem-solving skills that make them a good addition to any organization or team.

When dealing with them, you need to know that they might decide to push back at what you say, and they will also love taking charge, so you need to let them take ownership of huge projects.

Idealists

They believe in truth, and they form the biggest of the four temperaments.

They have a high value on integrity and authenticity and will tend to idealize their peers and colleagues. They usually put human potential in force at all times and have the capacity to help others to develop and grow, something that gives them total satisfaction.

So, how do you speed read an idealist? Because they have an idea of being the best in any argument, you need to be cooperative with them and helpful. When it comes to doing something, don't compete with them. You also need to be sincere when dealing with them; otherwise, you will lose their trust.

They are very creative, which means that you can take advantage of this creativity to help solve the issues that you have at hand. You also need to make sure you appreciate their contribution, and you will see the best in them. They are also very willing to help, and therefore you need to ask for their help at all times.

Chapter 3: What You See is Not What You Get?

You have heard of the phrase "what you see is what you get" being thrown loosely around in various perspectives.

However, you need to understand that this isn't always the case.

When you start speed-reading people, you will notice on different occasions that what someone portrays when you first meet them isn't what will come out when you get to know them.

Some people show you're their type through their feelings while others tend to hide them. It is upon you to find a way to explain these feelings. However, not everyone you come across will show you that what they feel is genuine; some will pretend just to impress you.

Since the act of perception is an internal process, and you need more than a few interactions for you to gauge the way they behave. The truth is that you won't be able to decipher what someone is all about just because they have specific traits. For instance, the mere fact that someone works out each day and has lots of money doesn't mean they are so strong on the inside.

When you look at a model, you might think that they have self-discipline and are mentally strong on the inside. Well, they might have that and more, but even if it takes a lot of dedication to push the body to the limit, some of them are weak inside.

It might be that these people might spend hours in the gym just to remove the self-loathing that they feel. Weight lifters might be perfectionists who always think that they aren't good enough, so they come up with a way to look more appealing.

You might see someone on Instagram with thousands of followers, only to realize later on that the person lives just for the likes that she receives on the platform.

This means that you can never know what motivates someone by simply checking them out.

For instance, you will never know the kinds of behaviors a person is going through until you listen to them. There are people that will get out the bed just to battle depression, and the mere fact that they have left the house is the biggest achievement ever.

People can be Strong in Some Areas and Not Others

You will realize that someone might have a combination of traits while you think they have a specific trend in your mind.

Well, the ideal trend might be the dominant one, but for many people, they have a combination. Some people are strong in some areas and weak in the other area.

For example, your boss might be the strongest in the workplace, yet when you reach home, you find that they have to overcome a lot of issues.

Additionally, people have the capacity to thrive well in some environments during a struggle in some. You might find them strong in some weak areas, but they are weak when you need them most.

How do you tell someone's Dominant Trait

While there is no way to see someone then decide whether they are strong or weak, you need to consider various aspects of their behavior.

For instance, you need to look at how far they are willing to go to better their lives. Some will sit and wait for the situation to improve, while others will go for exercises that will help them grow better. The good thing is that everyone has room for improvement at all times.

So, unless you have the capacity to know someone well, you might not realize how much effort they are putting into everything to make themselves better.

You might think you know your neighbor or friend too well when you are very mistaken.

Verbal vs Non-Verbal Communication

To begin, let's refresh ourselves on what nonverbal communication is and how it works. When we think of communication, typically the first thing we think of is speaking. Speaking is definitely an important way for us to communicate, but most of the communication is going on around the words being said. The words actually account for very little. Communication is the act of sending or receiving information between two or more individuals, and this is not always spoken. By communicating, we're able to share knowledge, lessons, and skills. This information is shared in two major ways: verbally and nonverbally.

Nonverbal communication, then, is quite simply all the kinds of communication we conduct without words. This includes actions that are both happening at a conscious and an unconscious or subconscious level. This might be the clothes worn by the communicator or the posture with which he or she stands. It might be facial expressions and gestures. There's even nonverbal communication present within verbal communication, such as unspoken communications like the speaker's tone, pitch, cadence, volume, timbre, register, or even their silence. Every little piece of information which is not directly said is nonverbal communication.

Where you might be able to control and even stop yourself from what you say, most nonverbal behaviors are largely involuntary and thus quite revealing. It is only when we study the art of deliberate communication that we begin to gain control over those largely involuntary behaviors.

It's critical to understand that most of a person's opinion of you is derived from the nonverbal communications you broadcast. The words you speak have very little to do with what someone thinks of you. If you've been rehearsing a speech over and over in order not to mix up your words, you should consider how much more beneficial that practice time would be to make adjustments and controls to the nonverbal cues you're sending.

When an individual says one thing, but their body says another, the audience picks up on this, either consciously or subconsciously. Impressions, opinions, and decisions are made based on this information. If the visual or physical doesn't seem to match the verbal, we instinctively recognize that something is amiss.

In various studies, scholars agree that the very words you use in your speaking make up only about 5% of someone's opinion of you. The nonverbal voice cues you're sending will make up for about 45% of an opinion of you, while a whopping 50% of the opinion consists of your nonverbal body language communication.

Keep in mind that this is an approximate measurement for face-to-face interaction. Written communication operates a bit differently, and while writing, communication does incorporate many of the same nonverbal elements, it must be observed and measured separately.

With so much of an opinion being formed on communications other than our words, it doesn't seem so strange to spend more time practicing the nonverbal parts of your speech, than the words themselves.

Nonverbal Communication – Then and Now

It was only in the 1870s when we began to question nonverbal communication in any significant or scientific way. The idea of nonverbal communication was raised with the publication of Charles Darwin's third major work, The Expression of Emotions in Man and Animals. It was in Darwin's observation of nonverbal communication between animals that it was considered among humans. Today, the study continues and expands.

Understanding and using nonverbal communication today is more than scientific observation; it's a profession. There are many professions that bank on their nonverbal communications to lead the way and set the profile.

When it comes to guiding and inspiring other professionals, knowing a thing or two about nonverbal communication makes all the difference. Keynote speakers take the stage to inspire sales teams. Trainers and coaches hold students accountable for reaching the goals they've set. Whether to inspire a sales team, a singer, an actor, an athlete, a parent, or a student with important exams, coaches are always working with their clients' patterns of thought and behavior.

Not only does Tony Robbins attest to deliberately using deliberate nonverbal communication on himself, and within business and social situations, he teaches others how to do the same. Tony Robbins is a very well-known American author and life coach who regularly hosts or speaks at seminars that cater to a wide variety of individuals. The audience is often comprised of business professionals, entrepreneurs, and other driven individuals wanting to accelerate their success and develop themselves on a professional or personal level. He also speaks on the theory, the how-to, the virtues and results of a lifestyle augmented by reading individuals and communicating in an influential way.

Robbins, along with many other coaches and speakers at a local or national scale, teaches individuals how to use verbal and nonverbal language and behavior to assess and therefore influence interactions. Learning the art of reading and broadcasting both verbal and nonverbal communication puts you at an advantage, allowing you to command an audience with confidence. It allows you to say just the right, impressive, things at the right time for that romantic or financial prospect. It allows you to move more freely through a host of social situations you'll inevitably find yourself in at some point or regularly.

For coaches that guide sales teams and entertainers, teaching others to project themselves deliberately is one of the primary functions. So much of what we do is a psychological game more than anything else. No matter if you speak to a king, a saint, or degenerate, the inherent senses that emotion plays upon is an equalizer. We are all human. We all want safety, food, and shelter. We all desire to be of value and to be loved. We all strive for self-actualization.

The art of analyzing others acknowledges this and utilizes it to elicit a particular response from the individual or the public. The desired response comes as a result of the harmony between the language of the actual body and language.

Name another professional that distinctly adheres to the philosophies of deliberate body language and verbal language—attorneys and lawyers; especially trial lawyers. Trial lawyers routinely represent clients in significant court cases, arguing in their client's support and defense. Without a doubt, this requires a keen sense of how one conducts himself in the courtroom. It requires a deliberate intention to build a conscious and subconscious rapport with the jury and judge. A trial lawyer must also guide the client to deliberate body language and deliberate speech for the best possible results in the trial.

Nonverbal and verbal persuasion is used to build a rapport with the judge and jury. It's important to be able to read the body language of the jury in the initial stages. It provides insight to the lawyer about which areas of the trial of the story need more attention, emphasis, or avoidance.

The way a juror might fold their arms, rest their posture or the micro-expressions on their faces provide an indication of that individual's mental and emotional workings at the time. In addition to reading the individual jurors' body language, the lawyer must know what's needed to broadcast themselves as sure, confident, and authoritative. This is not done by facts and words alone, but by the way in which one carries him or herself, the way in which one conducts himself or herself on the courtroom floor. All of these factors are weighed by the jury, either consciously or subconsciously.

The lawyer assesses the jury and their nonverbal communications to make a determination about the best way to tell the story. The lawyer can then change the tone, cadence, volume, timbre, and register of voice during certain points throughout the trial, to add influence and persuasion.

Without the skills to read the jury's body language and expressions, the judge, the witness, the opposing party, and the client, there would be little control over persuading the jury. Without these skills, the lawyer would not be able to serve better, the client in defending his or her rights. Reading the nonverbal communications of others, and broadcasting your own nonverbal communications deliberately, are both fundamental tools for this profession.

In the business world, a negotiator's role is to ensure that maximum value is felt by each counterpart. To achieve this, negotiators must read, interpret, and communicate in a deliberate and tactful way. In most cases, a rapport has been developed, and it's at this sometimes-stressful point that the relationship is most fragile. The wrong phrasing or timing and the rapport which has been built could collapse. The negotiation could go sour and result in an indefinite delay or a withdrawal of interest. To avoid this, negotiators employ a series of tactics to maintain the interest of their counterparts and to demonstrate high value.

One of the primary ways to read and influence your prospect is to actually listen to what your prospect is saying, both in their language and in their body. If you listen carefully, instead of just waiting for your next chance to say something brilliant, you'll actually pick up on clues and tidbits of information that you can use later with your prospect to persuade them.

An example of this might be a sales professional trying to close one of the biggest sales so far. In an attempt to demonstrate value, the sales professional prepares a PowerPoint presentation of all the major features and functionality that will surely impress the prospect. However, when the sales professional listens to the prospect closely and carefully, it becomes clear that the prospect is only concerned about one major aspect: customer service. The sales professional could go one of two ways.

If careful listening has been applied, the sales professional will realize the PowerPoint presentation of features, and the functionality they've prepared is virtually useless. Just the prospect wants to trust that the sales professional will be responsive and supportive; the skilled negotiator with focus on this. If the professional has not listened carefully, the plan is probably still to try and dazzle the prospect with the PowerPoint presentation of features, which will ultimately lose the interest of the prospect instead.

Another fundamental skill of a masterful influence in any interaction is to come prepared if possible. If you're headed to a job interview, do your homework first. Look up the company's website online. Get familiar with it. What topics were recently covered in the company blog? What services are provided, and at what cost? We can see how the ability to read body language and other nonverbal cues plays a large part in negotiation. These are only a few of the fine professions that make a living reading the communications that others are broadcasting. These individuals' success can be the success you experience from your own application of these tools.

Types of Nonverbal Communication

With so much information packed into nonverbal communication, it's probably not a surprise that there are many forms of it. These very common behaviors below fall into three main groups.

The face communicates very often through:

- Eye contact
- Eyebrow movement
- Smiling
- Fake smiles
- Lips
- Wrinkling the nose
- Facial expressions

Facial expression is the main way we communicate emotions without the use of any words or noises. Facial expressions are universal in nearly every case. No matter where you go, you'll see the same facial expressions to convey emotions of surprise, fear, disgust, anger, sadness, and happiness. You may notice that facial expressions are very often used in conjunction with other verbal speech and nonverbal behaviors in order to make as clear a display of emotion as possible. This is evident in the dramatic example of theatre actors and the like using exaggerated expressions, body language, and gesticulation, in order to make it clear to the audience what the character is feeling - and better yet, what the character wants other characters to think he feels.

The body communicates very often, though:

- Hand gestures
- Posture
- Body orientation
- Body language
- Space and distance, or proximity
- Touch
- Personal Appearance
- First impressions

The perceptions others have about you are largely drawn from how you hold and carry yourself. Body language and body movement give others ideas about you, whether they are conscious or unconscious of decoding this information. This could be the posture you keep when you walk in the room, when you stand to speak, when you cross the street, and when you meet someone for the first time. Consider your clothing and appearance and the extension of body language. Surveys indicate that most people judge an individual based on their appearance in less than 3 seconds. Among the most popular elements judged first are the shoes someone wears, the hairstyle (including facial hairstyle) someone chooses, their clothing, and the hands, including nails.

Paralinguistic communication very often consists of:

- Humor
- Silence
- Symbolism
- Sarcasm
- Tone
- Volume
- Pitch

Paralinguistic are bits of information communicated with sound, and with the vocal cords in particular, without actually being words. This could be a gasp of fear, a sigh of relaxation and contentment, or a groan when a terrible smell is encountered. This also can include using elements of conversation subtly, such as humor and sarcasm. This could also be the myriad ways an individual uses the voice while communicating words. When a speaker changes pitch and tone, there is a recognizable change in the decoding of that information. When a speaker speaks loudly and then whispers, it elicits a different response from the audience in each case.

Shaking Hands

Another component of body language that is often overlooked, but truly deserves its own attention, is the handshake. Unlike facial expressions, the etiquette and expectations of a handshake can vary from region to region. Some handshakes are fast, and some are slow. Some are aggressive, and others are soft. Some deliberately impose a subconscious signal to assert dominance, and others seek to show compassion and ultimate respect. Some handshakes should not be made unless the two individuals are of the same gender. In still other cases, the handshake can be seen as cold and callous, where a closer greeting such as hugging or kissing, might be more appropriate.

But all of these examples, under analysis, are revealing critical information to you. Whether for personal reasons or socially imposed ones, some information can be derived that hints to whether the person feels confident or shy; entitled or unworthy.

Handshakes as a social behavior seem to go back at least to the 5th century BC and have been depicted as communication of greeting, congratulations, and particularly, agreement. In almost every case, the handshake is taking on the whole to symbolize honesty and respect between the two individuals. We see this in sports, politics, business, and in customs, like shaking the hand of a newly married groom.

In some parts of the world:

- Men are more likely to shake hands than women
- It's appropriate to shake a woman's hand before a man's
- Children shake hands when meeting
- A firm shake is rude
- A kiss is part of the shake
- Both hands are used
- A soft shake is a sign of respect
- The handshake is held during the entire conversation

All over the world, in communities where handshakes are expected, there are individuals who do not want to shake hands, and furthermore, are afraid to shake hands. In some respects, this makes sense, as the fear comes from that of contamination and not necessarily connecting via touch. Some individuals, though, do not physically like the way it feels to touch others. For whatever reason, someone has, they may not want to shake hands. In many cultures, this has been taken as a sign of disrespect, and certainly, there are still many regions that observe it as such, but in the modern world, and especially in cultures where business and commerce takes precedence, we become more accepting of skipping the shake and bonding and building rapport in new ways. Sometimes we might see this as the elbow bump (and similar shared gestures like it), which seems to be an acceptable compromise somewhere between making contact and not making skin contact.

Another part of the handshake that is often overlooked is the eye contact that goes with it. In most cases, you should make appropriate eye contact with the individual when you shake their hand. A handshake that includes eye contact conveys honesty and truth. Likewise, a handshake that includes one or both individuals avoiding eye contact is a sign of mistrust and deception. Keep in mind that both the handshake and eye contact, could be getting encoded deliberately, but then, pay attention to signs of deception and lying.

Next, we'll take a closer look at how parts of the Limbic system and the mind affects the way we react and respond.

A young student has worked over 20 hours to complete a 40-page essay for her college class. She then had to develop a visual representation to accompany her presentation. After three restless nights and countless cups of coffee, she is finally ready to present her finished report to the class. After performing an engaging and educational discourse, she breathed a deep sigh of relief. After class, she approached her professor and asked him how he enjoyed it. Barely looking up from his computer, the professor stopped and said, "It was fine," in a monotone voice. She was devastated. After dedicating all of her time and resources to this project, she was not satisfied with, "It was fine." A week later, after wondering what she could have improved upon, she finally got her grade back.

Shaking, she opened the link and saw a 100% grade. She was ecstatic. She felt greatly accomplished and proud of her work. However, she still wondered why the professor gave her that response if he was going to give her an A.

The professor could have genuinely loved her presentation. In fact, it could have given him chills. However, because he was so monotone in his response, the student grew insecure. He gave off the impression that he did not appreciate all of her hard work. In reality, the professor greatly enjoyed it; so much so, he gave her a perfect grade. What is the issue with his actions?

Likely, you would conclude that the way he uttered, "It was fine," was a turn-off. That monotone delivery is quite different from the excited, "It was fine!" paired with a clap. This is the power of verbal communication. Although one person may say one thing, the way they speak it reveals the truth. Our body language works closely with how we speak. A rather rude comment can be overlooked when paired with a smiling face, or it could be taken as extremely creepy. In addition, a smile can hide insidious intentions. This is why body language is a compilation of various components.

When a person constantly speaks in a harsh, assertive, and bold manner, others may conclude that that person is angry. They may even avoid associating with them for fear of embracing negative energy. In reality, the person could be amicable and positive. However, the way they place great emphasis on certain words or topics is intimidating. The power of tone, emphasis, and volume can create great conclusions when it comes to reputation. However, there are exceptions to this theory. Some individuals may express themselves one way, yet their actual personality is quite different. Take, for example, the late Michael Jackson. Michael had an extremely light and timid voice. He would speak almost like an unsure child, retelling a bedtime story. Upon only hearing him, one may conclude that Michael was submissive, shy, and quiet. The reality of his persona was quite different. The innovation found within his music and the creativity exuded through his dance moves illuminated great power and confidence. Despite the volume, tone, and inflection of his voice, he was a mighty lion when it came to his job. However, personal friends and family members knew that somewhere, deep inside, lived a submissive, shy, and quiet person. This denotes that within our voice, despite the intention, lie deep-rooted personality traits that we may be blind to. The loud and boisterous individual may be seeking to compensate for a deep insecurity. The arrogant and assertive lawyer may be fuming with angry emotions. The way in which a person speaks is complex and reveals truth.

The power behind how you say something can turn your innovative idea into a passed opportunity. Imagine pitching an idea for innovation with a monotone voice and no sign of excitement. Surely, those on the other end would not be convinced this is your passion. You may have missed your opportunity simply because you lacked enthusiasm. Your voice can also be a manipulative tool used to assert to others. There is a stark distinction between yelling rules and explaining them. The way a person says something can make a difference in how the sentence is perceived. A stressed manager can assert, "Why are you always late?" to an employee with a stern voice and a frowning mouth. Or she could kindly say, "Why are you always late?" with a slight touch on the shoulder and a concerned tone. This could be the moment where the employee either opens up or seeks further employment. When you think about it, words are just extensions of the mind. We all use them and express ourselves in one way or the other. However, the tone can drastically alter our perceived intentions and even our reputation.

The volume in which one speaks can ignite action. A whisper may indicate confidential information, while a loud yelp could signal, "Get away!" In addition, a monotone voice could indicate disinterest where an emphasis on words and syllables could signal excitement. Sarcasm, on the other hand, is quite tricky to decode as it is subjective to the person speaking. One lively individual could show sarcasm, in the same manner, they would offer a greeting. This is where contextual clues come into play. Analyze the person's body language. Do they have a slight smile or a straight face? Does what they say seem outlandish in relation to the topic at hand? Interpreting sarcasm involves integrative techniques to understanding. It is a complex system that is unique to each person. One of the primary reasons why sarcasm is so difficult to understand for some is because it can mimic traditional body language cues. In this respect, it may be essential to get to know the person you are speaking with, so they can better understand your personality. Then, little by little, bring on the sarcasm!

Understanding your personal inflection can affect your reputation. You may have the purest of intentions, but your diction, volume and choice of words are taken adversely. Others may create a distance between themselves and you due to this inconsistency. Being cognizant of the way you say something can be a true indicator of your intention. In addition, your communication skills will operate smoothly. The two main components of mastering effective communication are control and awareness. It is important to control the tone, inflection, and volume of your voice. It may even be necessary to control the type of words you use. Next, being aware of your audience, surroundings, and mood can play a huge role in how your words come off. A bad or melancholy mood may not be suitable for a children's book reading at the library. You can practice altering your verbal skills by seeking feedback from others. Have them analyze how you express a sentence, and they can provide constructive ways to improve.

Our Bodies and the Way They Speak

There are types of body language. This is because we cannot classify the different styles in the same category. Different body languages can be distinguished. So, which body language styles can be differentiated? Generally, the body language is divided into two columns. That includes; Body parts and intention.

So what kinds in each class can be observed?

Let us start with the body parts and the language they communicate:

- The Head - The placement of the head and its movement, back and forth, right to left, side to side, including the shake of hair.
- Face - This includes facial expressions. You should note that the face has many muscles ranging from 54 and 98 whose work is to move different areas of the face. The movements of the face depict the state of your mind.

- Eyebrows - The eyebrows can express themselves through moving up and down, as well as giving a frown
- Eyes - The eyes can be rolled, move up down, right, and left, blink as well as the dilatation
- The Nose - The expression of the nose can be by the flaring of the nostrils and the formation of wrinkles at the top
- The Lips - There are many roles played by the lips, that include snarling, smiling, kissing, opened, closed, tight, and puckering
- The Tongue - The tongue can roll in and out, go up and down, touch while kissing, and also the licking of lips
- The Jaw - The jaw opens and closes, it can be clinched and also the lower jaw can be moved right and left
- Your Body Posture - This describes the way you place your body, legs, and arms connected, and also concerning other people

- The Body Proximity - This looks at how far your body is from other people
- Shoulder Movements - They move up and down, get hunched, and hang
- The Arm - These go up down, straight and crossed
- Legs and the feet-these can have an expression in many different ways. They can be straight, crossed, legs placed one over the other, the feet can face the next person you are in a conversation with, they can face away from each other, the feet can be dangling the shoes

The hand and the fingers-the way that your hands and fingers move is powerful in reading other people's gestures. The hands can move up and down, they can do some hidden language that only people of the same group can understand.

How one reacts to handling and placing objects-this is not regarded as a body part, but it technically plays a role in reading body language. This may predict anger, happiness and much more.

This includes willingly making body movements, otherwise known as gestures. These are the movements that you intended to make, for example, shaking of hands, blinking your eyes, moving, and shaking your body in a sexy way, maybe to lure someone, and much more. There are also involuntary movements—these are movements that you have no control over. This can be sweating, laughter, crying, and much more.

Importance of Body Language

Most individuals rely on social networks and texts to connect in the modern digital age, and this is a very reliable way to do so.

While digital communication enables people to speak at convenience and can reduce stress on certain individuals, something can be lost in so doing, and because you are incapable of recognizing the person when you speak to them, you can miss key non-verbal signs in addition to verbal ones such as vocal inflections. Digital communication has become the main method for people around the world, and to satisfy this, there is the likelihood that body language will proceed to develop. Most of the time, you may hear the negatives of body language. Maybe you are told not to twist in a certain way, sit this way or that way. However, body language can influence your life positively. Let us look at what you should do to maximize body language.

How Body Language Can Influence Effective Communication

While we may feel and wish that interaction is as easy as the phrases that we say, it is not the truth. The reality is that our message is heard more than just our words. If in an email, text, or instant message you've ever been mistaken, you know what I'm talking about. Words alone are not enough. Body language is part of what strengthens and wraps up the message and if individuals see us as face-to-face or use video cameras, our body language influences our message and presentation. You may find that body language helps the receiver of information read your mind and interpret your thoughts. Acknowledge that there's more to the message that you're sending, there's the meta-message of who you're and the intention to send that message. Body language is constantly communicating to your audience.

My aim in this is to offer you some specific advice to help your communication in the body language that you use and to increase the chances that your message will be heard and understood properly.

Always Make Eye Contact

It is first on the list, without a doubt. You will be surprised to note that, our eyes talk more on our behalf. However, this is prone to some cultural differences. We develop confidence in what we say and believe the other individual once we make eye contact. Our eyes may be the portals to our soul, but they are certainly a way to develop a relationship and provide effective communication. You may say that you are shy and unable to make eye contact most of the time. Well, the shyness may cause you to look down or sideways while communicating. Your audience may interpret this as a lack of confidence in your message. I would advise you to nurture your eye contact. The good thing about body language is that you can learn it with time—purpose to develop the skills step by step.

Walk Energetically

Picture the first time you meet anyone. In a sluggish posture, they come to you, ambling towards you. Picture the same scenario now with an individual walking with intent and power—we're not thinking about sprinting, but a deliberate walk. This mere act is the individual's opinion, isn't it? Our walking style sends out a message of trust and authenticity and also beauty. When you walk in confidence, you depict that you know what you are up to and believe in yourself. You know what happens next, people will be able to believe in you too.

Bring Out a Reflection

Our feelings and considerations appear through our non-verbal communication, which is the purpose of this article. When you need to discuss better with others, consider reflecting on their non-verbal communication. This isn't a YouTube snapshot of an infant emulating another person, the fact of the matter isn't to copy or ridicule somebody, yet rather to show sympathy through your non-verbal communication. This must be inconspicuous and will take practice; however, it can enable your messages to be gotten all the more effectively by others.

Give Individuals a Chance to See Their Hands

We as a whole utilize our hands to convey a message. You can even watch individuals on the telephone, when the other individual can't in any way, shape or see them, utilizing their hands to present their meaningful conclusion! At the point when individuals can't see our hands, they wonder on the off chance that we are concealing something, if we are anxious, and maybe numerous different things. Your hands are a piece of your effective communication; so, use them and maintain a strategic distance from any negatives that may originate from concealing them from others.

Utilize Empowering Non-Verbal Communication

Two quick models: eye to eye connection is referenced as of now, and gesturing with individuals to show that you comprehend and additionally concur. When somebody does that it conveys capably to you, isn't that right? This isn't the main model. Identified with reflecting over, this utilizes our body development and motions to show individuals we give it a second thought and need to tune in to and gain from them and that what we are sharing is to their greatest advantage.

Slow Down

A few of us speed up our communication. It is advisable to slow down, however, it hinders your signals and development. While some speed conveys vitality, we cross an almost negligible difference that leads our non-verbal communication to show tension, apprehension, or even contemptibility. Take a full breath and relax a little bit.

Have an Incredible Handshake

If you have one, you realize how significant this is. If you are unconscious of this reality, you might just have a limp, dead fish, or overwhelming and over-controlling handshake. A handshake communicates something specific about what your identity is. Work on a firm and welcoming handshake, and you will impart believability and certainty to other people.

While we as a whole can and should deal with these things, perceive that the beneficiary of our message, the watcher of our non-verbal communication is the judge. Their view of our non-verbal communication runs the day. At the point when we apply the thoughts above, however, we will improve the odds that their discernment is certain and will bolster better correspondences and connections.

Have you ever met and struck with a perfect stranger? It almost seems as if you have met before when you find plenty to chat about. It just felt okay. You talked about almost anything, you lost track of time, and you felt so relaxed. You formed such a good relationship with that person that you knew what he'd say. All clicked between you, and you felt really close to this man. It could have been a physical attraction or just on the same wavelength. You thought your thoughts matched, and you enjoyed each other's time. This is a relationship. When there is a friendship with someone else, we may vary in our views but still feel a connection or a partnership with him. There can even be a friendship between two people who share a very little resemblance.

Either we realize it or not, we are read cover to cover by others continuously. Even without words, the body's language speaks volumes. Body language is often an unconscious thing. It is not necessary for us to make a diligent effort, through all the details, to think about why one has just folded his arms across his chest and narrowed his eyes to us. The unconscious interprets this behavior immediately to suggest opposition, distrust, even though we have not observed the opposite individual or his context.

So much about you, be it visible or subtle, tells someone else something. The words you use, your facial expressions, your hands, your voice tone, and your eye level will determine if you and your message are accepted and/or rejected. To be convincing, you have to be not only open but also authoritative.

Everybody's confident for a living. There is no way around it. There is no way. If you are a salesperson, an investor, or even a holiday home mother, you will continually be left behind if you are unable to persuade others to your own way of thinking. Get your free Success Advantage reports to make sure you're not left to watch others take you on a successful road. Donald Trump said it best, "Study the art of persuasion. Exercise it. Develop a sense of its profound value among all aspects of life." Fifty-five percent—(body language) visually 2. 38%—vocal (voice ton) 3.3. The full use of body language does not only involve mastering your own use of outward gestures to establish and maintain relationships but also means gains in the capacity to read another person's body language. If you can read the body language effectively, you can recognize other people's emotions and discomfort. Tension and disagreement can be seen. You may feel dismissal and suspicion. You must understand that the language of your body adds or diminishes your message. In other words, your subconscious actions and expressions can help or damage your ability to convince others. You will report by knowing and adopting the correct corporal roles and heads.

Touch is another important part of the language of the body. Touch can be a psychologically, very effective technique. We want to be treated subconsciously; it makes us feel loved and valued. However, it is true that we have to be conscious and careful about a small percentage of the population who do not like to be affected. But in most situations, touch can help to make people more comfortable and open to you and your ideas.

Touch can give the person affected a positive perception. Touch is the perfect transmitter of immediacy, love, similitude, comfort, and informality. For one research study, librarians made one of two items when they gave university students library cards to check books: they either didn't touch the individual during the exchange, or they had light and tactile contact, placed a hand on the student's palm. The students who were impacted during the transaction generally viewed the library system more favorably than those who were not affected. Waiters who touched customers in their arms asking if everything was all right were given greater tips and judged more positively than those waiters who did not touch their customers.

We recognize that certain parts of the body may be affected openly, while other areas are out of bounds. Women do not care that they are touched by other women and are fairly tolerant of being (appropriately) touched by men. Men don't usually mind being hit by an unknown woman—but things get more difficult to predict if men touch other men. People don't like to be approached by foreign men in general. The healthy touch areas include the elbows, forearms and hands, and the upper back occasionally. All this depends on the pre-touch situation and relationship between the two parties.

Touch often encourages consumers to a particular store to spend more time shopping. For one report, salesmen's physical contact led customers to buy more and to make a more favorable impression of the shop.

Another example shows that the number of people who have volunteered to collect papers, sign petitions, and return money has increased. Hornick found that touching bookstore customers on his arm led them to shop longer and buy more than customers who had not been influenced to judge the store better. Hornick also found that supermarket clients affected were more likely than untouched customers to taste and purchase food samples.

Analysis Persuasion is the final piece of the puzzle that breaks the code to increase your income dramatically, boost your connections, and allow you to get what you want when you want and win friends for life. Tell yourself how much cash and income you lost due to your failure to persuade and control. Think about it. Think about it. Sure you saw some success but think about the times you can't do it. Have you ever had a time when you didn't get your point through? Were you unable to convince anyone to do anything? Are you fully realizing your potential? Can you motivate yourself or others to achieve more and achieve their objectives? What about your connections? Imagine facing challenges, realizing what your intuition thinks and feels, being more confident in your ability to convince.

The Psychology of Body

The word ' body ' evokes many images, others more esthetic, religious, or even medical. On social, personal, and psychological aspects of the body that define identity, interaction, and emotion. The human body is perceived differently, and that explains how indifferent or concerned we are with our bodies. For example, some monks live in the Himalayas sometimes without clothes or food and skeletons. Likewise, a few women in trendy communities may like to live with minimal clothing and food, but the whole intention would be completely different in both cases, of course. The monks are attempting to move beyond the body and attempt to understand the purpose of their lives by sacrifice, while most body-conscious people are physically attractive. We see that similar behavior can have very different objectives, and it is funny how different people perceive the body differently.

These days, men and women are dressing up and showing their bodies for all manner of reasons-protesting against global warming, making money, giving money to charities, protecting the environment, and even selling cars. Philosophers deny that the body is so necessary, only as a means to convey a personal/interpersonal identity. Nevertheless, the body is an important aspect of art, culture, and society, and in modern times, the body needs a psychological perspective.

I will attempt to build a philosophy of the body with three things in mind: 1. Body Image–That's the perception that gives us a sense of identity; 2. Body Image. Language of the body–It is the body's main social or communicative function and allows us to communicate with others and 3. Body Conscience–It stresses the relation between mind and body and mental dimension, which indicates the connection between our thoughts and our corporal reactions.

Therefore, the body is above all a tool by which we recognize ourselves and others. Our perception of our own bodies or bodies of other people is directly related to the image of our bodies. The image of the body is our perception of form and size and is essentially about our physical appearance. The body defines our identity, and we project ourselves into the world through our bodies. Yes, we are the brains; we have no other name. The body image dictates whether or not we like the body in which we are trapped. It's almost like we are stuck in one particular body. To develop self-confidence and a sense of inner beauty, a positive corporal image is required. A negative body image will decrease body appreciation, for example, in young men and women who are increasingly concerned about excess fat and lack of muscle. People try to develop muscles, and women try to reduce their weight based on the social perceptions of appearance, which directly affect the body image. However, the human body can be viewed from the anesthetic, an erotic, or a medical point of view.

The way we perceive our body depends on how we perceive the corpses of others, so our negative image of the body is largely driven by our own idea of a perfect body. If an obese girl considers that a woman with a slim tail has the perfect body, she will naturally develop a body's negative image. The portrayal of our bodies, therefore, influences our personal life, our way of life, and our emotions. While physical attention should be encouraged, an implicit concern about the body's appearance could be detrimental to a person's wellbeing. Given the huge importance given to nudity, cosmetic surgery, a perfect figure, beauty competitions, and such problems in most urban societies in modern times, there are naturally numerous discussions and questions about body image. Psychologists and sociologists should decide how far men and women should follow their corporate interests and whether the body element's public enthusiasm should be limited.

This naturally brings us to the body's other important function: the interactive element and its role in communication. The body's language is just as important as verbal language in communication, and the interaction between two people is mainly based on nonverbal communication. The body language signals are often sometimes even more relevant than what the verbal language tells us. If your girlfriend tells us that she loves you, then this is verbal communication. If she also shows hidden interest in other men, it is non-verbal communication, which may be equally important when determining whether your girlfriend truly loves you. The body is an important communication agent—our eyes, lips, hands, actions, positions, and movements determine how we think and feel.

The facial expression is also as important, and we sometimes try to understand a person rather than his words. So, if a person praises you when you least expect him, you may want to see if the person is genuine in his praise or simply sarcastic in his face. When the verbal language is misleading, the body language gives truth and true feelings and intentions. The body is an interface with an individual, and the body language is a social aspect of this interface and an important part of our social life and everyday communication. Turning your eyes away while you talk to a person can lead to discomfort, and hands-on the tail can indicate an attack. In certain cultures, some body positions may be offensive, although some standard corporeal postures and movements are common across cultures. Therefore, our bodies' language is about our sense of identity and how we preserve this identity and connect with society.

The final part of this discussion is about body awareness, and many recent studies have shown the way stress experiences can influence the physiological mechanisms in the body in relation to the relationship between mind and body. For example, higher blood pressure was observed in people who were invited to take part in stressful events such as dangerous sports and even cultural activities such as theater. Developing strong emotional wellbeing requires regulating the body by the consciousness of the brain. When we are "aware" of altering the body because of anxiety or any psychological changes, we can also regulate the brain so that our biological processes are not adversely affected. Controlling the mind with the body or the body with the mind by exercise or meditation or other pressure reduction/relaxation techniques can, therefore, help maintain a balance of the mind-body that is absolutely essential for a healthy life. Although many people understood the relation between mind and body in ancient times, this is a very recent discovery in psychology. In psychology, cognitive psychology, and medical psychology emphasize the mind-body connection, and research initiatives in psychology on the mind-body connection are only in the early stages.

The body is an important aspect of our existence, and almost all of our existence has to be defined. It gives us a sense of identity by emphasizing body image, provides us with social skills, and helps us communicate with others by means of body language. Nevertheless, through the mental and essentially spiritual dimensions of mind-body contact, we gain consciousness and understand how the body can be used for a broader relationship with the mind and even the world beyond the calculation of physical attractiveness or social interaction. Finally, being human means not just being in the body but also moving beyond the body and its limits in order to fulfill our greater purpose of life.

Bodily Gesture

Facial Expression

The expression facial (also, facies, face), with the eyes, is one of the most important means to express emotions and moods.

Through knowledge and observation of facial expressions (that is, the moving face and not as a static object) we can get a better understanding of what others communicate to us.

We also make judgments about people's personalities and other traits based on what we see in their faces. For example, people with attractive features are often attributed certain qualities that they may or may not actually possess.

Not all communication that is transmitted through facial expression is susceptible to being consciously perceived by the interlocutor; however, it is known that the impressions we get from others are also influenced by the imperceptible movements of their verbal communication.

The face and first impressions

In the first meeting between two people, the initial five minutes are usually the most critical period. The impressions formed in this short space of time will tend to persist in the future and even be reinforced by subsequent behavior, which is not usually interpreted objectively, but according to those first impressions.

Since the face is one of the first features we notice in a person, it can clearly play a vital role in the process of establishing relationships with others.

In these few minutes, we form opinions about their character, personality, intelligence, temperament and ability to work, their personal habits, even about their convenience as a friend or lover.

Chapter 4: Body Language and Its Benefits

Nonverbal contact plays a very important role in our everyday lives and interactions with others. It needs careful communication to determine a positive relationship and maintain productive relationships with our mates, employers, and relations.

If we do not follow the foundations of excellent visual communication, we are going to reduce our name and landing probabilities into better opportunities drastically.

Improper communication leads to broken encounters, incorrect first impressions, and deceptive choice of words.

This book offers some strategies for cultivating subsidiary communication and a host of effective and elegant ways to express yourself in public.

Confidence   Relaxed   Trustworthy   Strength

The communication isn't close to the movements of the hands; however, it is also concerning in the way we are while standing. Positive communication is additionally a requirement not only for conferences or structured conversations, but also for events, teams, and different reasonably meetings or experiences that we've got an inclination to partake in on a daily.

Body language is characterized because of the non-verbal contact between two people or a community of individuals via physical actions like limb movements, facial expressions, eye movements, and body gestures and postures.

Today, the word has gained such plenty of significance and recognition altogether aspects of existence that any person can thrive within the skilled environment, personal lives, and within the universe normally, without meaningful communication.

Not only through regular talks, but also through structured debates, seminars, cluster conferences, council conferences, etc. Not only does smart communication transmit the right assuming to the receiver, it often draws or repels the receiver.

For example, you have a chunk interview, and the interviewer is interviewing you. Now, while you're polite and address the questions correctly, the interviewer doesn't like you. The explanation for that is terribly evident. Your body posture or body movements may not be acceptable or rude. This might have a semiconductor device for the questioner to assume that you are not fascinated by the task profile. Otherwise, you do not seem to be an honest candidate.

Visual communication, however, differs from sign language. Language or material is freely communicated in language through hand and finger gestures. Throughout language, typically, lip gestures, finger motions, hand movements, and eye movements are used for transferring information to the communication receiver. However, within the indisputable fact that communication is largely involuntary and not actively controlled by the mind, communication is totally different from signing. Sign languages, however, are voluntary and are regulated by the mind so as to expire data.

Visual Communications

The following are the vital options of body language:

- The body sections are a group of accidental acts
- Requires movement, in particular of the limbs and ears
- It lacks descriptive linguistics

- Different people have to be compelled to interpret that generally

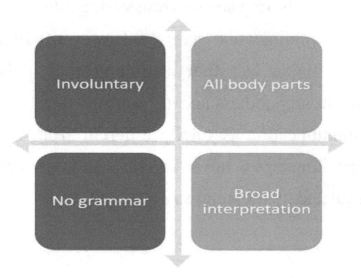

Languages

Here are the key options of sign language:

- The deliberate movement of body components isn't a way of transfer info
- Has the science of its own

- It's a clear significance rather than a situational context

It will not mean that it cannot be regulated if communication is unconscious. One can quickly develop one's visual communication by practicing those strategies described during this text, and by carefully analyzing one's body movements at every time.

Body language is a style specific to a selected culture. In several cultures, what's accepted in one culture is a big 'No.' Also, visual communication is not standardized and may even be obscure. For that reason, this guide teaches you the basics of good communication.

What's Positive Body Language?

People find the vocabulary constructive engaging, open, and fast to tackle. A supportive language of the body must place us in a very place of security, modesty, and likeability. This allows us to be clear and approachable to other individuals, permitting them to feel relaxed as they convey with us. When the reverse is expressed through our body gestures but, thus, our visual communication isn't constructive, then it must be modified.

- Visual communication isn't meant to be aggressive. Defensive communication stops individuals from becoming concerning about us and forming a bond with us.

- Visual communication doesn't convey a way of tolerance within the various parties, because it'll contribute to career loss, conferences, and standing conferences.

- A human visual communication must be neither dominant nor submissive, but assertive in expressing our thoughts and mood in an exceedingly very positive way, without insulting the other person.

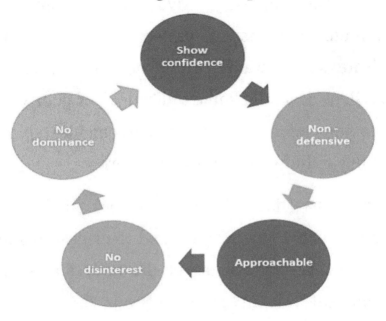

Positive communication allows people of a group or culture to be accepted by other people different from them; it is also good or necessary for people of different origins and ethnicities because it plays a crucial role in influencing our conversations and interactions in our daily lives.

Importance of Positive Visual Communication

In these intensely dynamic surroundings, communication is of utmost importance. The private sector wants sturdy communication, an excellent deal, and some indications of poor visual communication can interrupt agreements, typically leading to individuals losing network.

A previous adage claims, "Acts talk louder than words." Our body position and their gestures and positioning varied areas of the body and play a significant role in expressing our thoughts and emotions, whether or not we've got an inclination to don't consciously express the emotions.

Assertive Behavior

Positive communication helps the person to be more assertive and helps to express his or her opinion simpler than the others. Some individuals like positive communication, and thus the person with a positive visual communication gets more recognition and support in each speech

Nonverbal Communication

Studies suggest our discourse is comprised of 35% verbal contact and 65% nonverbal communication. It means one thing we are saying freely amounts to solely 35% of what the alternative person expects. The remaining 65% of data about us is learned from the language of our body. Our communication helps others to identify our emotions, standing, and fashion as well.

Nonverbal contact, along with language, plays an important role. Our nonverbal communication is capable of reiterating our argument, contradicting our language, reinforcing our purpose, removing the sense of our sentences, and complementing the sense of our phrases. Since nonverbal communication will either underline or contradict our purpose, we'd wish to stay our communication in sync with our emotions. Some proof of communication disagreement with our vocabulary can make us appear untrustworthy and discomfited.

Geographical Point Success

In offices and business cultures, constructive communication is a must. Healthy visual communication will cultivate the spirit of work at the job and might conjointly raise workplace productivity. Delegation of duties through constructive visual communication is a bit complicated. This might conjointly serve to specify feelings towards workers and overcome social disputes.

During business conferences, one must use corroborative communication to demonstrate curiosity, acceptance, and excitement, a fragile smile, soft hands, forward-leaning and eye contact can honestly contribute to developing respect for the other party throughout the discussion, therefore, serving to develop and sustain a positive interaction with the other participants during a cluster.

Relationships

Negative visual communication could crumple to abundant confusion and mistaking. A relationship is often destroyed by keeping a body cause and ludicrous body gestures that are disrespectful to the other individual.

For example, you would like to grasp the opposite person's emotions and mood, and you need to tailor your behavior; consequently, if the partner is in a very good mood, then it's safe to joke or taunt her generally. Also, if the partner isn't in a good mood, an analogous behavior could even be misinterpreted as satire or irritable behaviors. It can produce conflicts for partners and might conjointly end in broken relationships.

Speaking

Body language takes on a really new aspect, which suggests once it involves speaking. Whether the person features a protecting communication or a neutral visual communication, there's a high probability that the observer doesn't reply to him or her intently. The resulting rate of these speeches is so lowered by a major proportion because the observer receives 35% of the actual correspondence.

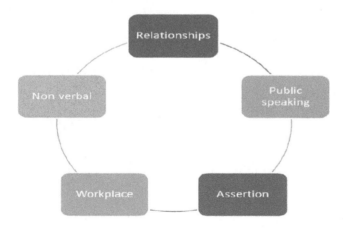

However, it lacks the remaining 65%. Therefore, possessing correct body motions to associate a degreed stance once standing on stage with an audience is necessary. For each mode of communication, the communication is a variety of relevant. This helps break down the stigma of unusual and helps produce a stronger link with the knowledge receiver.

Sensible Standing Postures

Much of the time, we tend to encounter men; we tend to stand in front of them. If it is a spontaneous encounter on the road or acknowledgment of somebody within the point or enjoying a conversation at a celebration, all the discussions that arise in our lives occur when we are standing.

The proper postures to use while standing up for a discussion are:

Stand Erect

The initial thing to consider is to face with a straight neck. The back must be straight because this provides some way of being tall. The subsequent size typically makes a positive impact. You should not slouch or hunch.

Hunching or un-erect posture creates a degree look of lethargy and laziness. If you appear frail or languorous, an individual won't want to approach you to speak. Humans still favor positive behavior. Wrong standing conditions typically symbolize poor self-esteem. Bad standing is not a positive attribute of the sport.

Face the Person

The second issue to note is not to make the audience look horizontally. Seek to pose face to face with the person you act with. Standing sideways indicates you'd just like the individual to hurry and do not want to begin chatting. Look out for the opposite person's same signs too. If that person stands sideways, please stop speaking as soon as possible. This may be due to the alternative person not being interested in auditory communication.

The sole thank for arising is to guide your face towards another person. Ensure the center meets the opposite person's face with no intervention in between. Standing with your arms crossed over your chest may be a big 'no' too. Crossed arms symbolize protecting or introverted nature. That kind of mentality is never accepted by men and is throwing off different men.

Free Your Hands

The third thing that has got to make sure is not to position your hands in your pockets when you speak to others. The stance shows contempt. Holding hands within the pocket suggests an individual isn't concerned in speaking. Keep in mind that the arms are visual communication vocal cords and may speak loudly about your mood and wish.

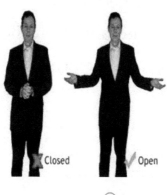

Closed   Open

Look to the Eye

The fourth thing to take care of is viewing the opposite person's eyes without threatening him or her. If you keep gazing away from the other participant, your interaction could indicate a lack of interest. Continue looking at the alternative person for these signals too. Sometimes, perhaps the alternative individual is facing far away from you. That's likely to mean the person isn't inquisitive about you, so it's better to let the individual go.

Move Your Limbs

Last but not least, bound limb motions are sensible. Within the aim, raising hands indicate your involvement within the discussion and, thus, your level of enthusiasm. You'll be standing, excluding the thighs too. You shouldn't use your fingertips to twiddle your face, because it symbolizes timidity and loss of trust. The hands won't be crossed, in fact. Crossed legs symbolize confusion and barred existence.

The Proper Handshake

Handshakes are the associate's totally necessary side of our lives. Day after day, we see acquaintances and coworkers we are able to greet. The handshakes are as ancient because of the culture of man. In Roman days, the custom of engrossing the lower arm was practiced as a technique of testing that the alternative individual carried a knife underneath the sleeves. Little by little, this developed into a form of traditional acknowledgment and then, step by step, reworked into the contemporary day's handshaking.

Shaking palms are stuffed with dos and don'ts. You'll rarely give a hug to a stranger. Handshaking could also be an image of obtaining individuals invited. When you're unsure of whether or not you're accepted in a place, it is best not to enkindle a handshake. Salespeople are also seen taking charge of this when meeting a replacement customer. Instead of introducing a hug, they switch to a quick head-node. A handshake isn't meant to mirror superiority or obedience. All it is extremely showing is dignity. Let's take a quick glance at those and their characteristics.

The Equality Handshake

It's perceived as a hidden, symbolic power struggle between you and the different people you greet. In brief, any of these participating within the handshake won't face down or approach.

The palms of all the individuals are in a vertical place for honest handshaking. Instead, the two people can apply analogous energy. Once you notice that the pressure you add is higher or that of the alternative individual, then you'd wish to alter the intensity of the impact.

The Submissive Handshake

The submissive handshake happens when the palm faces forward and lies underneath the other person's arm. It's "palm back drive," and you are feeling submissive. Don't let the alternative guy have a handshake on his favorable position.

The Dominant Handshake

The superior handshaking is that the reverse of submissive handshakes. It happens as you place your arm over the opposite person's hand, then the hand faces downwardly. That's named "pull down the arm." This handshake conveys your power and superiority. Don't make the universe believe you're dominant just because your hands are dangling over the opposite person's hand.

The Vice Handshake

The vice handshake is another handshaking that's usually loathed around the world. The handshake is achieved by poking a palm out, so aggressive hand gestures follow a defense of the hands of the opposite party. The strokes are thus rough that the individual providing such handshaking looks to be overly commanding and powerful.

The Tip Handshake

One of the scary types of handshaking is a handshake with the palms. The two persons actually contact each other's fingertips during this form of a handshake and provide a rather tiny stroke, or may maybe skip the stroke. This handshaking conveys the loss of vanity and lack of trust. It's slightly usually found throughout work interviews. That sort of handshaking throws off the enquirer simply before the conversation ends, and also, the interviewee's experience goes for a flip.

The Straight Finger Handshake

The individual handling the hand has all his fingers straight during this type of handshake. Not clasping the opposite person's hand may be a really poor and disrespectful act; as a result, it indicates a lack of confidence in meeting and repulsion towards the other person. Often note to grip the opposite person's hands and provides it an honest stroke during the handshaking.

Correct Hand Movements

Hand gestures, in fact, are somewhat automatic. We tend to show us plenty concerning the other one that uses his or her hands when they communicate, although. Additionally, within the case of hand expression, there are pointers for constructive communication.

Release Your Palms

The first concept is to still leave a palm wide. Open palms indicate transparency and approval. Release palms say integrity and legitimacy too. However, there are thanks to deciphering the open palms too. If the hands are open when talking; however, looking downwardly, this means the person's stance could be a little authoritarian.

Unless the palms are extended, though, and face aloft, then it is a non-intimidating warning. This individual is friendly and, in essence, is going to be said as welcoming. Palm spinning, then, totally changes the approach individuals read them.

Uncrossed the Limbs

The arms shouldn't be crossed while communicating, and also, the palms should not be grasped. Grasped hands prove a lack of dedication and lack of assurance. The arms crossed represent a protecting or tense posture. It was also found that if a person is standing with arms crossed, they are even less likely to cling to the interaction with the associated open-armed person. As compared, protective communication often ends up in lower staying capability.

Don't Hold Your Limbs

You should not cross your arms while talking to others. This can be a symbol of vulnerability. Please stop waving your arms crossed in front of the crotch region because that also always indicates vulnerability. It's named the location of the "Damaged Zipper." This could be a cause that at the same time shows vulnerability and obedience and, this should be avoided at the slightest degree prices.

Don't be too dynamic with your limbs in front of an audience because it reveals again that you are just annoyed, you are anxious. The ladies can remember that they're not going to hold their arms next to each other when they chat because it demonstrates their protecting stance and dangerous existence.

Nil Limb Barriers

When you are having a conversation in an exceeding restaurant, be sure to hold the cup properly while you are talking. If you are speaking to a special person, there should be no limb obstacle. Keep the vocabulary of the body-free, and hold the cup in one hand.

Crossed Legs Etiquettes

Legs remain hidden from our heads, so there are high risks we'd forget them throughout our conversations. We tend to try and do relay lots of details concerning our thoughts and reactions all the time, although.

Hands and head gestures positively lead to the observation of constructive communication. Though, legs have their own worth and have to be compelled to be controlled in applicable places. Let's examine what various varieties of crossed legs mean.

The Standing Leg Crosses

The standing leg cross is also an indication of resistance, sensitiveness, and submission to the core. This is the angle voters tend to take when they encounter someone who is a total stranger.

The standing cross of legs symbolizes a lack of entry to the genitalia. This will be the reason that on balance, this cause is known as protecting. Such a movement then indicates the individual isn't self-assured or, in numerous terms, lacks self-confidence.

To ladies, it indicates she must participate within the discussion; however, it is refused entry. In men's situation, that is when more implies the guy must participate within the talk, but he still wants to be sure he isn't at risk of everyone's exposure.

Therefore, while anyone seems nice in speech communication and has snug facial expressions as well as correct hand gestures with crossed leg posture, please notice that the individual isn't as positive or happy as he or she is attempting to appear.

When an individual in front of you talks honestly to you and additionally has that perspective, it is better to let the individual feel very comfortable. It's because the individual just isn't as confident communicating with you as he/she presents you.

The Double-Cross
The double cross appears when the individual is crossing both the legs and also the pinnacle. That shows the individual is totally bored chatting with you. These people aren't sensitive to spoken language, thus either establishing a quick relationship with them or quitting is less complicated.

Figure Four Leg Clamp
The individual locks one leg over the other during this cause and puts his hands on the elevated knee. This action indicates the individual becomes absolutely impartial towards us and becomes stubborn in perspective. This gesture often implies

the individual is unsentimental and refuses to price the opinion of others. Even his own thoughts hassle him.

The Mortise Joint Lock
The individual locks the ankles along during this cause. The hands are squeezed in a very mitt or placed on the bottom, or even grab a chair. This movement indicates the individual is suppressing a particularly negative feeling; appreciate anxiety, concern, or doubt.

This sort of communication is typically associated with people inactive with an offense or created with hearing in an exceeding case. That's one cause that could even be stopped.

The Leg Twine
Each of the legs is raised during this cause and then wrapped around the different hip. It's an indication of timidity. That one action is only for women, which symbolizes vulnerability.

Parallel Legs

It is one leg posture individuals must follow. It's scarcely ever seen any man replicate it. Such cause offers individuals plenty of strength an improved and more assured feel that sends forth a powerful feminist image. This leg cause reflects a corroborative communication, motivation, and vitality and is deemed the strongest feminine leg cause. This also gives the ladies a young feel.

Dominant Stand

It is one pose wide seen within the military by men and girls. The person spreads the legs apart during this position, and also the feet are set firmly on the underside. It's a dominant cause. Such a stance could look nice and dignified within the armed services, but usually, it'll even appear threatening to bound voters; because it'll sound imposing for the individual taking a commanding position.

Attention Position

This cause is typically acceptable in circumstances wherever an individual who is also a junior in rank encounters a senior in rank. The cause doesn't make categorical any temperament to stay or leave. Thus, this posture shows that the person is neutral to matters and has no closed or negative views.

Do's and Don'ts

Caution should even be taken whereas sitting. Many people rest by flipping the chair around and leaning over it by inserting the chest on the chair's back. It's done specifically to demonstrate that the individual occupies an area and makes a shot to be assertive. However, it offers off a very opposite impression. This pose shows that the individual is not comfortable and tries to protect himself/herself by building a buffer between them and others.

Foot skipping remains a significant downside for various people having to be operated on. Recurrent foot banging against the bottom is also a reflex symbolizing frustration and impatience. As individuals wait to collect, take a glance at findings or diagnostic records or one thing that's substitutable with lots of confusion, they still faucet their foot unceasingly.

The legs must be uncrossed and straight for work interviews or community conferences and also the foot should be planted squarely on the table. If individuals are in community meetings, they'll cross their legs within the shape of a customary leg cross, so it is a big 'no' for men to try it. Inserting legs and feet plays a very important role in emotional transference signals and being chosen at work conferences and community conferences.

Pleasant Facial Expressions

Most facial expressions do the task of convincing the other person of the information. The standard person cannot be able to perceive legs or arms visual communication. But nearly everyone can read the signals that appear on somebody's face. This can often be of utmost importance that we tend to preserve a sturdy and appropriate countenance, must others blame the North American nation for being unapproachable.

The initial gesture everybody in an exceeding person is trying to find is the smile. Smile is also rejuvenating but at the same time frustrating. A woman with a tight-lipped smile that does not show teeth is, in fact, indicative of her lack of involvement within the discussion, whereas it'd seem to a standard person that she is inquisitive about this speech.

An Original Smile vs. a Pretend Smile

An initial smile has multiple characteristics regarding it. Wrinkles are formed around the eyes any time a person smiles impromptu, without any voluntary power. That's because the lip edges are drawn back in an associate initial smile, and therefore the muscles are contracted around the jaw. Solely movements within the lip arise in an exceedingly false smile. Those that provide false smiles simply smile through their mouth and not through their eyes.

So, what if the person you're reproofing tries to form a false smile by choice wrinkling his or her eyes? This even includes a method to classify this. If a smile is real, the fleshy portion of the eye between the ear and the palpebral is shifting inward, and also, the ear ends are usually subtly dipping down.

Studies have found plenty of personal smiles, the foremost support he/she gets from the others. This can often be another characteristic that implies they pretend smiles. If a person tries to imitate a smile, the proper brain hemisphere—the one that focuses on facial gestures—simply sends messages to the left side of the body. And a false smile on one side of the face would still be brighter and softer than the other side. However, both components of the brain transmit messages in an exceedingly sincere smile, and thus the smile on either side is equally powerful.

When the person's eyes draw back from you, therefore you've to know that the individual is annoyed with you, so it is best to either alter or avoid the topic of the conversation. Once the lips are tightly squeezed, though, the eyebrows are lifted, and there is an unbroken look of eyes at you along with the highest upright or gently force away, this implies the person's curiosity in you.

Positive Communication – Walk Smart

A heap of information is distributed not only by the way you stand and speak but also by the way you walk. The walking vogue conveys plenty of knowledge regarding our authority and mannerisms. This can often be one reason why their students are educated on walking methods by the communication coaches.

Stand Erect and Confront

The initial thing you'll bear in mind is not to slouch or hunch whereas walking. The back should be straight, and also the spine must be erect. The highest must keep straight, and also, the eyes have to address the forehead. The chin must always be up.

The bulk watches down whereas they walk—that is not considered beautiful. Additionally, if you slouch or hunch whereas walking, you will be considered weak and lack energy and enthusiasm.

Poor posture while walking can contribute to back pain, sore neck, and different serious ailments if maintained for prolonged periods of it slow.

Pull Back the Shoulders

The next thing in-tuned in mind is to flinch the arms and relax. Having a pushed back. However, snug shoulder posture helps produce a strong and upright pillar, whereas your progress. This kind of walking, combined with the straight back and lift stance, tends to reduce accident probabilities. Even this stance tends to exude confidence and energy.

The upper part of the body always desires to return into action beside the legs while walking. To make confidence, the arms should swing properly. Once you continue walking, the limbs can travel in smaller arcs. The faster you walk, the longer the arc tends to be. The arms activity helps reach a quicker speed.

Get the Right Pace

Quite a ton depends on the speed of walking. When walking, the speed should be so that you can just greet a person adequately while maintaining the walk and don't constantly seem out of breath.

Being wise always involves not taking too several moves whereas you walk. Prolongation of the gait overly strains the muscles of the legs and contributes to steering destabilization. Studies have shown that there is a method of sex-appeal connected with the touch swag of the shoulders.

The knees must be straight whereas walking and also the moves should be of comparable length. You've got to increase your body to the hip at ninety degrees and correctly walk on the choice leg. It allows balance while walking. The elbows can reach upward and then tuck the pelvis to a lower place in the abdomen. Additionally, the top mustn't be bowed and should be unbroken erect. Last but not least, put the feet on the initial underside and not the foot.

Positive Communication – Correct Eye Contact

In any communication or contact, eyes are very important, which suggests that if the language of the eyes goes wrong, the complete discussion and, therefore, the person's credibility goes wrong. Eyes speak a message unavoidable within the eyes of another.

Eyes contact controls dialog and comments regarding obedience and domination. All people take into consideration once they initial bit is the eyes of the other. And thus, all parties involved create easy, eye-based judgments regarding each other. Hence, the eyes are the instrument for conveying information on the perceptions and feelings of others.

Let the North American nation have a peek at each of the eye-borne texts.

The Dilating and Catching of Pupils
The pupils get expanded once anyone gets excited and may probably dilate up to fourfold the primary

scale. Conversely, the pupils seem to contract once an individual is upset or in another unpleasant mood. So, if you notice that the pupils of the alternative person have dilated, that indicates the individual is fascinated by you or your chat. But if the pupils have contracted, it is best to understand that there is no worth within the boy.

The Hair Flash

In nearly every society, the short rise and fall of the hair convey an extended distance "hello," it's the show of the nose. The eyebrow's blink of an eye movement is also an approach to greeting each other. This includes an uncomplimentary connotation in Japan, though, and thus, it mustn't be shared by Japanese voters.

The Game of Eyebrows

When speaking, raising the eyebrows means surrender. In contrast, lowering the eyebrows implies superiority. Those that intentionally raise their eyebrows look submissive, and other people who lower their eyebrows are sometimes remarked as hostile.

There is one stop. As women drop their eyelids and at the same time raise their eyes, this transmits sexual obedience. So, this term should be discouraged in each structured context.

It is additionally suggested that a person maintain eye contact with the alternative party to express concern and purpose. Once you keep viewing the alternative individual for an extended time, though, which can place the opposite individual at any inconvenience, your gaze can harass the alternative guy. In most societies, it has been determined that the attention can match the attention of the opposite individual for around sixty percent to seventy percent of the time to determine a healthy relationship with the other individual. Once you start viewing them with curiosity, the other people can assume you appreciate them; then, they're going to reciprocate in their eyes.

The Sideways Glance

The sideways glance is also used as an associate sign of curiosity or perhaps hostility. If paired with a smile or subtly raised eyebrows, a sideways glance might signify curiosity and is often a typical image of appeal. However, it'll make categorical skepticism, disapproval, or perhaps hostility if the sideways glance is paired with a frown, downturned eyebrows, and downturned lips.

The Magic of Blinking

The pace at which the eyes blink is also a strong information conveyor too. When you're involved in chatting about anyone or one thing, you're not going to raise your eyelid as much as possible. When you are not involved with anyone, though, the danger of move the eyes can raise drastically. Increasing the blinking pace of the eyes conveys fatigue or neutrality.

The Dart

If the opposite person's eyes start darting from one side to the opposite, it means that the person has lost interest in you and is trying to find routes of escape to induce to eliminate you. This shows vulnerability on the other side.

The Authority Gaze

Another approach to exude power is to lower your eyes, raise your eyelids and concentrate tightly on the alternative. This offers exposure to what predators do before they strike their victims. The blinking rate should be reduced so that the other person's eyes must remain continuously focused.

A significant side of our listening skills and even our communication is eye contact and facial gestures. Hence, keeping honest eye contact with the alternative party is of utmost importance, while not threatening him or her. Eye communication plays an enormous role in promotional negotiations, work reviews, and even informal interactions.

Positive Communication – Mirroring

Seeing others can be a method we tend to value more to determine connections with others. Proof conjointly noticed that those around you feel a variety of drive to perform identical behavior as others love. Assume you're sitting on a footpath. Suddenly you pause and still look upwards. This will be not unimaginable, and also to determine that the voters who imitate you will continually pause their speed and appearance up to the celebrities. A variety of the most common sorts of mirroring is the yawn.

This type of mirroring triggers a yawn within the others and also as men yawn. Another sturdy mirroring illustration may well be a smile or a joke. Once a person starts to smile, it becomes so contagious that the others around them begin smiling too. Mirroring is another excuse that enables people to navigate well. If a person is in an exceeding line, he or she doesn't get unruly as others obey the foundations and do not interrupt the queue. It's quite the outcome of 'symbiosis.' A study showed that people opt to make more mates while wearing identical ways with each other.

Mirroring helps you feel reception around others. It is, thus, thought of as a significant method for establishing relationships. In fact, once somebody starts to mirror you, it shows that the person is in the set with you, which ones he likes your business. An ingenious way of gauging somebody's level of interest is to try and do some action and observe whether or not the other person imitates you. The analysis shows that girls are more inclined, instinctively, to mirror alternative girls than men to mirror alternative men. Often, people don't seem to mimic other women much, even while they're in a courtship mood.

Evidence suggests the girl considers the guy more fascinating, compassionate, and pleasant when the guy resembles another individual. It leads to people possessing a completely different desirableness. Men take into consideration it troublesome to imitate somebody, and also the mirroring behavior helps people feel happier. Mirroring will usually be observed as we tend to work out people in an exceedingly long association. Once people detain longer relationships, they start trying similar and behave equally. Mirroring usually displays a love for each other. Mirroring plays a giant role whereas talking. Persons are going to be mirroring the opposite person's speech, rhythm, delay, and tone throughout a discussion.

Knowing Regarding Nonverbal Communication and Visual Communication

Nonverbal communication takes place while not using language. Visual communication can be a branch of this communication that focuses mainly on the body's numerous gestures and, thus, facial expressions.

It doesn't look like anything at first. Does someone explain something without using words? Will you claim "I love elephants" without being verbalized?

But apparently, there is a lot to be mentioned about the unsaid.

All variety of information is gathered from:

- Facial expressions
- Gestures
- Posture
- Touch
- Tone of voice
- Rate of speech
- The volume of physical voice appearance
- Stress of voice
- Personal space
- Clothes
- Hairstyle
- Hygiene
- Engagement with others (such as how long do I keep eye contact)

Perhaps on a subconscious basis, we tend to know and use this non-verbal contact—you do not know yourself—I'm going to itch my nose now or imply why you're doing that. Once one thing happens, you still don't know.

Why Hassle Regarding Body Language?

In the analysis of communication, the aim is to become more aware of this "dirty" communication and learn the way it functions; that's all. However, we tend to speak and interpret and react to varied behaviors. It's regarding keeping contact under control. Don't you wish to grasp a way to deal better with social interactions? Or feeling other people's moods and emotions going from their behavior and gestures? Consider it as a chance to develop your social competencies. It is not about doing makeovers and temperament changes. It's a chance to know your social environment and acquire the 'know-how' to handle it better.

If you'd wish to be more convincing, the very best reasons given below are why somebody must worry about nonverbal communication and body language:

You will Connect with People Effectively

So, many people are worried regarding speech and understanding, and thinking at any given moment concerning the price of this will profoundly impact your life.

There is proof that 60–93 percent of our connection is through communication, depending on that study you consult. Most of life goes around worrying regarding what to undertake and do and not whether or not to attempt to copulate. Learning communication can enable you to properly communicate with others because it can encourage you to spice up your communication skills. Once you may obtain on little movements, the alternative individual will assist you higher perceive them and contribute to deeper communication.

Fosters Your Business

Particularly if you're a variety of entrepreneurs, learning communication is crucial. Recognizing and adjusting properly to the language of one's body will make or break your company. Suppose you're in an exceedingly prospective shopper meeting, and easily keep going together with your pitch. During the method, you neglect to note that your prospect is crossing his shoulders, interlocking his ankles, and shifting something down. Ultimately, you go forth with no contract once you felt you were doing a fantastic job. Training to know such body gestures throughout sales interactions also will profit you. Addressing the just represented communication could save the speech and save your deal. This might lead you to a great deal of money in the long-term!

It Prevents Conflict

There can be an explicit quiet communication that we tend to use when we're angry or upset. By learning nonverbal protecting communication and rage, you will be ready to acknowledge when your companion is angry before they intensify. Just imagine what number of fights or negative comments; if you had the proper insight into the communication, you will either stop or standstill in their tracks.

Sends Improved Signals Regarding Your Presence

You'll even consider your own appearance through talking regarding the communication. What kind of messages does one must place out? However, does one read others? What do they do regarding your posture? Once you start learning communication, you become much more conscious of your own body. How does one position their arms? When is your head atilt in conversations? What is that going to say, then?

Victimization Communication Awareness Can Assist

You to Perceive Your Own

Body language permits you the flexibleness to spice it up. Another vital issue to notice is that you can simply use that to manage how you act since you learn the way visual communication works. You will be ready to use flexible communication by standing up and expanding your chest if you are feeling slightly depressed, listless, or down. Get everything finished in two minutes. You're going to start seeing how you have your strength back and, therefore, the way you're turning into lighter. By strengthening your own communication, you will have an additional useful result not only on others but also on yourself!

It Reveals Your World

Do you ever wish to drive a specific model of car? Let's presume you're thinking of buying the new

Chevrolet edition. All of a sudden, you see them everywhere! They're parking within the house depot, walking past the geographical point, and then a colleague begins asking regarding it. Has the vehicle been unexpectedly priced again and again once you created your thought? No, under no circumstances. This may be the subconscious that has been trained to travel trying to find them, currently trying out any single automobile incident. Identical visual communication can happen. In everyday interactions, there are so many occurring that we do not want to say. People can send quite 800 nonverbal signs in thirty minutes.

You will tell your brain to actively grasp what to look for by learning visual communication, and you may be amazed at what quantity you'll be able to see. Once you begin to test communication, it's like looking at the world in high definition. You will still see an additional layer of information all of an unforeseen.

The Importance of Communication
Speaking Publicly

No one should ever underestimate the importance of visual communication once speaking and presenting publicly. Pass off the inaccurate vibes, and wind up shunning the viewers. However, you will be able to quickly win them with the proper communication.

Some people only want to urge their speeches 'over and done with' without offering expressions and visual communication much attention in any respect.

In short, visual communication is the strategy the body uses to express itself without the assistance of spoken words. This could be the mixture of facial expressions, emotions, and actions that convey what is going on in your head. Study yourself to determine whether or not you are feeling immediately seated or standing. What is the expression on your face? Are you smiling or scowling? Are you standing up or slouched in your seat? If someone is attempting to want a photograph of you straight away, what do you assume people would say regarding you supported your gift body language? Are they reaching to tell you to seem nice and approachable, or are they trying to counsel you are someone not to mess with?

Body language is also involuntary, implying you'll verbally believe it or ail one thing; however, the communication would tell the precise opposite. If you have ever wondered why visual communication during a speech or presentation has relevance, here's why: People may always want to sound optimistic; however, they'll tell otherwise with their visual communication. And, they're trying to say things like, "I'm glad and happy to be here," but their facial expressions and movements suggest they are not.

If you are somewhere and you are introduced to many new people, you will tell them that you are pleased to meet them. However, your visual communication says the precise opposite while not knowing it. Therein social condition, you may assume you've got performed fairly sensible. Nonetheless, in spite of everything, the people you only met obviously didn't think an excessive amount of you because they solely didn't sit right with something regarding your communication. The truth is our visual communication is ill-famed because it betrays our inner emotions. We'd not utter anything aloud; even we'd refute it. However, our communication would let the planet grasp that we actually accept something or anyone.

Importance of Communication in an Exceeding Presentation

When it involves conferences, there's the strength of visual communication to make one surpass or struggle. If we tend to check our communication and produce it to sensible use, we are going to surpass and lose if we tend to let our communication get stronger. It's a necessity to specialize in your visual communication, too, while you practice your voice. You will be calm, happy, and guaranteed on the day of your presentation that you've got what it takes to ace the presentation! Here, the reality with conferences is that there are continually two aspects when it involves visual communication. There's the communication of the host (that is you), and there is the visual communication of the group. Not only are you able to recognize the thanks to being an implausible interviewer, but you also need to feel compelled to be able to interpret and gauge the response of your audience to your delivery.

It is pretty vital to seek out the thanks to interpreting the gang. You do not want to be one of all those presenters who think they're doing an implausible job on stage after they bore their audience to death, in fact!

Conclusion

The first way we will begin to attach is by visual communication of our facial expressions, movements, and postures as we are older. Even after we discovered a way to talk, this nonverbal contact often exerts a powerful and mostly implicit effect on our experiences, strangers' primary perceptions, and our own perceptions. There has been an issue of whether visual communication in infancy is natural or learned.

An inquiry on Olympic and Paralympic competitors was taken from over 30 countries. The researchers specifically studied judo competitors who could see and also the ones who had been blind since birth. Once they won, all athletes made similar gestures arms raised wide, chest out, head tilted back. But because the blind people had already been mute, such words might not be known. Another basis from which to suggest that visual communication is innate. Similar to people who can see when they speak, they have blind gestures. While some gestures are also pre-programmed, culture has an influence too.

The competitors who lost a match in the same study of judo athletes carried themselves differently, reckoning their homeland. Western competitors, where society encourages people to hide embarrassment, showed a more subdued reaction and didn't slump their shoulders frequently. Yet blind competitors from the identical Western countries bowed deeply in the loss.

The way in which you carry yourself influences how people view you and the way you see yourself. You ought to use visual communication efficiently to your benefit. For starters, imposing a smile will make running less painful and challenging. Studies suggest a smile makes it more bearable to stay on your side in cold water. Using your body alignment will facilitate you to feel better-off. As an example, standing as an adult female— beams apart, hands-on-hip, chest up—can cause you to feel stronger.

Immediately before an interview or athletic event, this so-called power pose could also be especially effective for ladies preferring to take a seat and fill in the way that takes up less room. Similarly, if you would like to persevere, cross your arms over your chest, and you may find it can facilitate solving a controversy.

In a study in 2008, students who were sitting crossed with their arms kept acting on an impossible problem almost twice as long as those with their arms at their sides.

Research often suggests that keeping a smile on others will make people believe you're trustworthy and knowledgeable. It may make people think you're an honest listener according to visual communication experts. The person who is speaking takes a look at the facial expressions and movements to make them feel more relaxed. One report from 2011 showed this to be a vital selling strategy. If you wish to let someone know you're listening, sit along with your whole body facing them, knees and shoulders pointing at them. So, if you choose to alleviate friction, turn your body subtly backward as things get hot, the full-on expression is confrontational.

Our nonverbal speech will repeat our argument, refute our phrases, affirm our assertion, override the sense of our sentences, and supplement the sense of our phrases. Because nonverbal communication will either highlight our point or dispute it, it's important to keep up our visual communication in line. A positive visual communication allows the person to be more assertive and tends to bring out his or her viewpoint more effectively than the others. The general public enjoys positive visual communication, and so the person with positive visual communication gets more respect and favor in every conversation.